# The Shaping of an "Angry" Black Woman

## Tamara Woods

SAKURA PUBLISHING

Hermitage, Pennsylvania

USA

# The Shaping of an "Angry" Black Woman

Tamara Woods

The Shaping of an "Angry" Black Woman

Sakura Publishing
PO BOX 1681
Hermitage, PA 16148
www.sakura-publishing.com

Ordering Information:
Quantity sales: Special discounts are available on quantity purchases by corporations, associations, and others. For details, contact the publisher at the address above. Orders by U.S. trade bookstores and wholesalers. Please contact Sakura Publishing: Tel: (330) 360-5131; or visit www.sakura-publishing.com.

Interior Editing by Pete Santilli & Derek Vasconi | Illustrations & Artwork by Dana J. Clark

First Edition

Printed in the United States of America
ISBN-13: 978-0-9911807-3-8
ISBN-10: 0991180739

# Thank You

I'd like to thank my family, and especially my mother. She would let me wake her up at 1 am with a poem when I was an angst-ridden teen and every word seemed too painful and immediate. She never told me that she needed to be at work in a few hours. She always listened. To my friend and artist Dana for trusting me enough to let her artwork stand beside my poetry. To Anthony for helping me to believe in myself, to my publisher Derek for believing in me, and to my friend Melissa, who showed me the fun in getting a little country, and was the inspiration for the title of this book. And for everyone in my life, who has supported me, listened to my poetry, and loved me. Thank you all so much.

# Foreword

As I've grown older, I've often been asked why I was so angry. At first I just ignored the question. I didn't feel angry. I may have been sitting silently, pondering some aspect of the world, and I would get asked about this anger. This anger that was apparently so deep-rooted that I didn't even know it existed. The older I grew, the more I was asked this question, the angrier I became. Why the hell do you always expect me to be angry? Always expecting me to go off in the grocery store because one of your stock boys keeps following me to make sure I'm not stealing some damn bread or at the tax office when I'm talked down to, like I don't know how to read. Soon, I wore anger like it was my favorite pair of Chucks, giving people what they wanted. A minstrel show played with black emotions rather than a shoe-polished face. This brings around an unspoken rule: The expectation of anger renders my anger invalid as it is my starting point, so it's not that important. This collection of poems takes a look at life, written over a fifteen year span of mine. It is flawed oddities, beauty foiled with ugliness. We are all more than just angry. Women are more complicated than just that.

# Table of Contents

**PART ONE**

1

**PART TWO**

23

**PART THREE**

49

**PART FOUR**

69

**PART FIVE**

97

**PART SIX**

12

# Part One

*Yesterday holds less offense,*

*if the smoke is dense.*

The Shaping of an "Angry" Black Woman 2

# 200 Cigarettes and a Box of Wine

When do I become the writer I'm supposed to be?

When my words drip off my tongue like a drop of cum left from the married man

who came over last night?

Or am I aiming too low

the drippings of my soul should splash on paper

like the grease from Mama's fried chicken?

Fill my arteries and choke them with love

so that my eyes will bulge, roll skyward

and... pause.


Perhaps the thing to do is to tell the world its coming doom

I should decide whether mankind's demise will take place

in 1 or 1 thousand or 1 million years,

but I can't see past my dog dying in the spring

and my daddy in the fall.

Are the words meant to put the fear of something

other than one's imminent death?

But I'm scared of seeing that white light

and what lies in wait for me.

And I do fear the reaper, but I don't fear the reefer.

Maybe that's my problem.


Maybe the true peak of my wisdom will come in threes,

Three husbands times three divorces will one day equal

two abandoned children and the time where my

mind almost splinters and falls through the cracks except I still have a

voice and it's loud on the pages but soft to the world outside my head and

so the cries of "Mommy play with me, tie my shoe, fix me something to eat,

Mommy where is Daddy, Mommy why are you crying?" will be flooded out by the

click, click, clicking of the keys.


I know I'm supposed to write these words, but I don't know the order yet and

how they should trip, stumble and fall into someone's mind.

The message is lost inside a paper bag beside a metaphor stretched too thin.

My power lies in the words that tremble on the tip of my tongue.

They wash up against me, stinging my eyes, leaving traces of misplaced

soliloquies;

they have the force of misspent youth, eroded dreams, stories

untold, unfold, pause to breathe, sigh slowly and reflect.

The words swell inside me.

They race helter-skelter and I can't form them in my throat,

articulate,

they crash against my mind's shores.

They're immense in their complexities,

elusive in their meaning.


200 cigarettes and a box of wine slow me down.

I am just my words' mistress and—

they taunt me and laugh at me with their fickle tendencies.

So, tonight this is where they've brought me.

Three steps outside of reality and a heartbeat from my own mortality.

The Shaping of an "Angry" Black Woman 6

# Laundry List

Gasp for breath,

The air makes that tooth throb,

Battery acid boils

over in socket.

Where's that clove juice that girl said could help?

Wait 'til income tax time

To get that pulled.

This ain't even a poem.

Just a list of the costs of bootstraps living.

The only way to go is

Up?

These boots squeeze my heels.

Limping through the system

Keeping me in the system.

# The Future is Now

From birth to social security numbers long.

Nine-digit barcode on the

Back of necks.

Life, your walking advertisement

Catering to your every need.

Pop-up ads of dentists and

Orajel on the bathroom stall doors,

Before you knew your tooth ached.

Drone attacks when obedience strays.

These are the days

Before the future

Collides with what we thought was future perfect.

When science fiction will work as a

Guidebook to reality

Instead of guesswork for its path.

The number becomes you.

# Art's Inspiration

Art fortifies, inspires

requiring other art to stand up and be heard.

Is there anything worse than a song left unsung?

The words unspoken.

Still locked in your throat's prison?

In youth I was sure my life was

half-way over before it began.

I thought alcohol soaked fists,

words dripping in angry rage would

do me in before old age got around to me.

So I wrote like there was no tomorrow.

Abandoning all hope for reason,

behind my prepubescent thoughts.

Before I could articulate it,

I knew I was writing for my life.

Because art needs a form.

It craves an audience like crack craves a stem.

Like oxygen craves lungs.

Waiting to be pulled in and pushed out, picking up

thoughts, interpretations, derision,

love along the way.


Barely recognized necessity

except to the plant who needs it to keep going.

They say art imitates life, but

Without art, there is no life.

# Be Wary of the Fall

It is a cycle that can't be broken.

Words left unspoken,

I will be the keeper of the key.

Slip into its slot

until time stops floating beside a memory,

extension of my existence

trailing like fire down my back.


Glare in my stare.

Caution rises as hopes plummets,

crashing into the wall.

Falling like the tears

dripping from my quivering chin.


Can't begin to find the middle

just wound up at the end

with wounded door

where my memories slip

out of my existence into a dream,

where I sleep to be free.

# Mental Abuse

Some like to have their words

roughly stuffing every orifice,

raw and bleeding,

getting gang-banged by thoughts,

Left a quivering sweating aftermath.

Others prefer a more civilized approach,

wooing words with picnic lunches in

a sunlight dappled park, Gingham blanket.

Hand-feeding them braised chicken

and bites covered in brie.

Soft discussions of love and families.


My words sit across

from me at the dining room table.

We haven't spoken in months.

Forbidden slash across his face.

He gnaws, mouth open,

his knife and fork pointing up to the sky

and his I-wish-a-ninja-would look in his eyes.

We've been like this for years.


And when the phone

rings during our sit down

time, my Words fly at me.

Scream through clenched teeth,

spittle splattered

against tightly closed eyelids,

because I don't want to see

that accusing finger under my nose.


Phone calls, emails, social media, bathroom breaks,

any interruption can trigger my Words,

angry refusal to stay and the resounding slam of the door upon
their exit.

Gotta walk real soft around him,

real quick.

He's like an alcoholic being roused from his drunken stupor.

A crackhead who needs just one hit.

A gambler whose desperation bets his car and gets ole snake eyes.

A lover who's trading me in for a newer model.

I'll never know when I find someone else in my bed.

With him.

# The Words?

Strung out night bleeds into afternoon.

Lipstick stains on unknown pillow,

Where the back of his head spells regretfully,

tequila shots were taken like water last night.

Too much of, too many of, everything.

Memories, like broken cigarettes,

taped together by vague notions.

Try not to slide on the vomit beside the bed.

Rise up envious night and let the day be dead.

Walk of shame game,

The remember his name game.

Eyes sting, trading thought for cigarettes.

The words?

One to Five. The jail bar blues.


Shoulders tense.

Can't convey... can't speak...

Clichéd metaphors trounce over truth.

There's nothing to see here folks.

When once poetry posed as my saving grace,

better than food, than great sex in exorcising my demons.

Escape.

It has escaped me.

My writing sounds like a child's,

Repetitive,

Thoughtless.

Where is that place inside of me where they lived?

The words?

One to Five. The jail bar blues.


My head feels too heavy.

Do me the favor of slicing through bones and sinew,

Look at the fibers of me.

Check my DNA for the alcoholic gene,

so every time I pick up a beer,

I won't wonder if this one will be the end of me.


Suck it down, flush it down.

And she said and he said, and

I couldn't say what should've been said.

She took pills like they were life's elixir.

One pill, five pills, ten pills more.

Those blues, those whites, those purples for sure.

Her yawning mouth hungry for oblivion.

Beg, borrow, steal, for just one-

Slobber down side of face, eyes roll.

Incorrect, incoherent, incapable of caring.

The words?

One to Five.

The jail bar blues.


Imprisoned by short sights, shorter visions.

Memories cut from this pill, that drink.

Yesterday holds less offense,

if the smoke is dense.

My shoulders are tense,

And I can't find the words.

He said,

and she said

and I couldn't say what needed to be said.

The words?

One to five.

The jail bar blues.

# Part Two

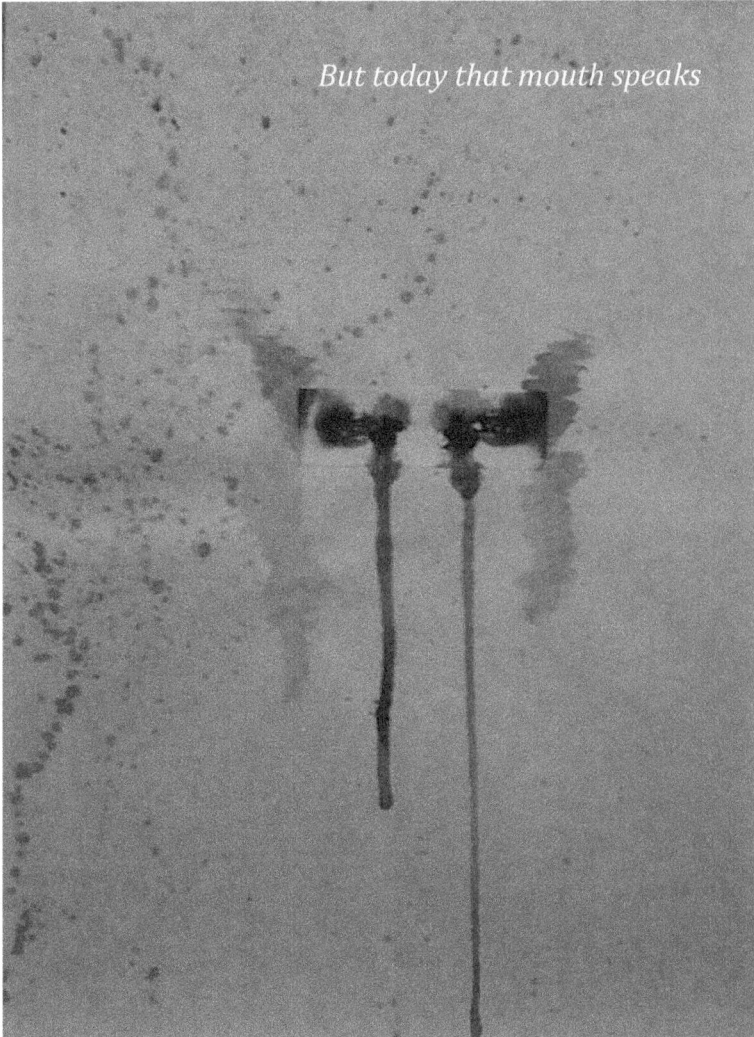

*But today that mouth speaks*

# Tongue-Tied

Black skin, darker than me,

Shining with cocoa butter.

Childhood acne pock marks.

Hair natural small solid puff, a little gray now.

Little grease in it, keeping it right.

Though his eyes were a little red.

Ain't nothing but that Ancient Age

they've been sippin' on all night.


But his mouth.

His mouth was a thing of horror shows and witches.

His mouth was open in a stickman's grin,

White strands crisscrossed over and over again,

Making a terrible netting for my unwitting soul to get caught.


Rude girl, you're being rude.

Couldn't stop staring.

The bullet my cousin had shot was lodged within.

I didn't understand the drugs and the lines crossed.

The fight and the police calls.

Hospitals stays, prayers that he'd be ok.

I only knew when he spoke, bubbles grew

And popped in the corners of the cave.

He sound like one of the ghosts in Scooby Doo,

But Shaggy wasn't there to save me.

I knew him, but I didn't know him.

He wanted a hug,

Fear held me still.

Didn't it hurt?

Didn't your heart ache because family is supposed to love and support,

Yours tried to kill you?


The devil lived in rocks in the 80s and it made its way to sleepy Fairmont, too.

Aren't your lips swollen from being forced into such a grotesque grimace that a child my size sees you as a monster?

I couldn't stop staring.

And he asked for a kiss.

# Insincere Flattery

I'm hating on that girl.

Her poetry and obsessions and pretense to care.

Does she know what it means to be free?

To be alive?

To feel so low that tears won't let you cry?

Why does she think she's everything he wants?

And you know, maybe she does.


Maybe he needs a pseudo-mom.

She can kiss his boo-boos after she kisses his dick,

And then makes him a sandwich.

He can stand a beer bottle on her ass.

She can pretend to be white trash.

He can dress her up,

use her up,

leave her wondering who she used to be.

Does a chameleon know its true colors?

I'm earth tones,

Oranges and reds shot through with the black of my reality.

Maybe she get on her knees and thank the heavens

above that she ain't sitting on the back of the bus with me.

She's driving in her car beside us, trying to catch a seat.

She can't be me, but she'll try.

She'll watch my moves and fake them,

It takes more than mimicry to replace me.

# Teen Cream Dream

I slept in it.

I marinated in the dream that

the wish would take me some

place beyond this space,

Where the sand meets high tide

and the spit flies from her angry lips.

She has become something more than me,

the entity of sanctimonious anger: fuck, fuck, fuck.

And her fists enraged little pistons railing against the world.

Smack, smack, smack.

I want to smash her face in.

She needs a hit,

And then maybe she would

roll into junkie-endured ecstasy,

leave my ravaged ears to be.

Or not to be.

Fuck that question.

Men's cocks turned tuning forks,

their vibrations tuned to her eyes,

wanting to spill their secret songs

behind her unbleached roots.

Women see her not The Madonna,

just the whore.

They send their men home

when she comes to town,

each one's chastity belt locked firmly in place.

And they are self-righteous in casting her as the villain.

Not even her unbent enthusiasm can break

through those steel-like chains of commitment,

her lust for all things long and hard will not destroy the ties,

the binding of love and fidelity,

Her thirst for salty emissions, or can they?

Does it matter?

They're just jealous.

Just fucking jealous.

Not everyone can go from being a

washed-out teen cream dream to a trailer trash meth

feen in a twitch of a tweaker's eye.

She would rather pack a bowl than face the truth of her consequences.

Her mouth is racing now,

One lie rolls off another,

her one-upmanship has taken on mythological proportions,

as she challenged anyone to dare be better

and she wailed over her Pabst.

Her ploy-autonomous pursuit of glory holes and grandeur,

Dickies and dicks

And Truth in destitution is why I left the path of spirit in her new man's hands

And I tried to down her bitter taste from my mouth.

The Shaping of an "Angry" Black Woman 34

# Tent Rape

Fumbling toward ecstasy, we were.

My breath caught in my throat.

It's all in the eyes.

I can't remember the name, he said.

I couldn't either and I cracked open

a Black label,

As if my memory hid at

the bottom of my dollar can.

I felt nervous with an innocence I remember

on my friend's face.

When I bought her first Playgirl.

Innocence I don't remember being.

He shook me,

But I wasn't ready to be shaken,

Not stirred.

Those eyes so bright,

Shook me and took me,

As more innocent that I remember.

I couldn't move.

I couldn't breathe.

And those blue eyes.

Narrowed in the claustrophobic tent.

I-can't-breathe.

And his breath on my face like acid wash

And I couldn't move.

Those blue eyes held the difference

Between freedom and losing myself

And as I cried years ago,

I cried into the eyes of this new blue-eyed guy.

I was fumbling toward reclaiming my voice,

What was the name of that album?

You look so sad, he said.

Of when it couldn't call for keeps.

And it's repeated Nos were ignored.

But today that mouth speaks.

# Coal Dusted Courts

It stops today, the inadequacy.

Complacency.

Not a victim.

Bloodline may not descend from the Mayflower

But it burned into the palm of balled fist of black power, my strength,

Gained through the backs of the bruised and battered.

Brown skin, tanned leather in the sun.

Brown skin, blackened in the mines.

Coughing up coal dust,

Chest rattling like a skeleton staggering

into chain link fences.


He gets his papers in,

He crosses every T. Dots every damned I.

That 20 years he gave of his life willingly,

To keep his family safe. Fed. Slightly ahead.

He'll get his reward now.

And his family will get taken care.

For those who are left behind.

And the doctor he say he don't have that Black Lung.

He's got a smoker's cough.

But he don't smoke.

This war has been lost.

Once standing proud and erect, life on the line,

Now he's pulling graveyard shift.

# A Kingdom's Decline

I don't remember the exact date

when the King died.

I do recall it was seven days after September 11th.

Tube was pulled.

He was gone.

His princes and princess paced outside.

The day's sun mocked the gravity of the situations

Or the rain ran like our tears,

One can't be sure of these things.


Killing ourselves one hit at a time,

Hoping the smoke would curl in our lungs,

we didn't have the fortitude for all the I love yous,

goodbyes and why weren't you better at this.

At least he hadn't abandoned his duty,

Right?

He reigned from the right end of the couch,

Remote in his left hand.

Asking for the royal sandwich or glass of soda.

Paunch growing in his inertion.

His Queen toiled day in and day out,

Reduced to servitude,

Those soft eyes filled with lassitude,

Sight weakening.

Lipstick can't hide

Disappointment's grimace.


The stars had aligned when they were four and five.

He'd known she was the one for him.

He'd wooed her into believing it too.

Potential for the love story of the ages here.

Instead reality's royal crown,

Had lost all its glimmer and gold.


Now the castle is in shambles,

The royal fruit rots on the branches,

Or flowers not at all.

It's cold there and dark.


When a King passes on,

The townsfolk and King's court

Discuss his supreme kindness and benevolence or

his malevolence, arrogance and pride

Rarely do memories allow for shades of gray.


Each King decides the conditions of his reign whether through action or indolence.

Attention to detail and duty.

# Provincial Providence

Her mass of steel gray curls

resting on top of her still regal head.

Her hands' shake slight,

cocoa skin still tight,

Like one of those 50 year young things who

dressed like the devil was her stylist

and temptation her fashion-designer.

Kids these days didn't know

how things should be done.

There's a right way and a wrong way to live.

And they were living wrong.

Her pocketbook slung over her shoulder,

a little perfume, not too much for the Lord's house.

She noted that the lavender complimented her skin,

but not with too much pride.

And the Lord, He would provide.

Didn't He take her out of the bowels of the Depression,

when Mama and Daddy could barely afford to keep them in potatoes

and ragged clothes?

Didn't He put her into Lester's arms,

who blessed her with five children,

a home for them to sleep,

and food for them to eat?

The sting of his other women had long faded over the years,

just like the bruises and the mended bones,

And the Lord, He would provide.


Didn't her children all grow to be so much more than she could've dreamed:

doctors, lawyers and wonderful mothers?

They had all grown and gone,

leaving her full nest emptied,

which she filled with church bake sales, socials, choir practices,

volunteers with the little ones on Sunday school.

And the Lord, He would provide.

The devil took Lester's heart before the drink did.

Didn't the Lord provide?

Didn't that life insurance help her to keep this house going?

Her coal miner widow's pension didn't hurt either.

Blessed are the meek: for they shall inherent the earth.

And the Lord would provide.

Even though sometimes in the quiet times of night,

When she was waiting for those little white pills

to take her into blissful slumber

and her mind wandered.

Speculating how her life could've been more.

If only she could've been the nurse that

she had wanted to be.

If only her parents hadn't agreed with Lester's that they would make a good match.

Freeing up some of their resources

having one less mouth to feed.

If only she would've had more pride.

Told Lester what him and his little wandering coal axe could do with themselves,

then maybe daughters wouldn't have turned out with a man like they daddy.


Except for the one who insists that her friend really is "just a friend."

They'd been "friends" living in the same house,

sleeping in the same bed

going on more than 30 years.

Like somebody got this old

by being a fool.

Her boys taking after they daddy

with the drinking and the women.

Lord, and the bruises too.

But the Lord, He will not tolerate

His people holding false idols including the bottle.

Now her beautiful daughter is lying in a bed of sin,

the sins of the father visited upon her.

She couldn't be faulted for her thoughts, could she?

What control did she have over them?

Less than the rest of her life.

Besides, the Lord He did provide her

the comfort of Pastor Brown's arms in these so-called

golden years.

Making the long dark nights a little brighter.

The Lord, He did provide.

# Part Three

*That's hard to swallow.*

# Just One More

Hopes and fantasies crashed against the shores of reality.

As the white bowl cools my hot cheek I ponder the ideas

of reality and fantasy--the here and now and what never will
be.

It's not just the one disappointment or the two,

Or the hopes of meetings that fall through?

So much more.

And so much less.

The eve of my discontent has nested in the pit of my stomach.

Mom's roast feels like it's going to give air soon.

The apple pie has maggots and I've never liked baseball.

That's hard to swallow.


I've taken to melodramatic deep sighs and misplaced "wows."

No reason, none I can give.

I can't explain the schism I feel separating me from you.

One foot on and one foot off,

Standing on the precipice between success and the abyss.

Consider this.

I've never been a failure.


When I was a mixed-matched black girl, who equated love with gentler fists

Every report card was heavy with As.

When I was a slacker-loser who smoked pot at 9 a.m. and then slept till 9 p.m.

I was being the best escape artist who'd ever touched a bong.

And when the malcontent disillusionment dressed me in its dark shroud

I became the most embittered cynic with an open smile.

Because I am nothing without contradictions.

And now what am I?

Good Christ, am I such a cliché that I have to resort to a Gen. Xer, "I Am..." poem?

I am somebody? I am a nobody?

Attention--

It has reached an emergency crisis status.

Should I lay me down, close my eyes in bed,

Tell the bill collectors, friends and family A. Woods is dead?

Go out tonight, cute hat on my head,

Find a hot stranger,

Give him some...


Let the loneliness bleed.

Call out the guards, ring my bell.

It's a long hot night in this short-lived Hell.

# Recessed Process

If it's penny for your thoughts,

The recession has raised the price,

But downed the quality.

Falling into a set of patterns,

Same syncopated response,

Stop, restart, repeat.

Ctrl+Alt+Delete

I've got the same blues

That everybody else do.

I got too much bills,

Not enough money,

My health's hanging by a peg and prayer.

There's nothing I can do but make this wish list.

Wishing all of this would go away,

And I could be free another day.

The Shaping of an "Angry" Black Woman 56

# Mathematics Atheist

I broke up with math in the 9th grade.

We used to add and subtract for fun.

Dividing up the world in ways that made sense

Multiplying by infinity and beyond.

Then you matured.

You added letters to your maths.

Being a word nerd, at first I was intrigued.

But these maths were foreign to me.

You wanted me to guess the value.

Why can't you just tell me, Math?

Why I got to come through your formulas to try to tease out an answer?

The problem was bigger than my bangs.

We had so many fights, that year.

I longed for the days of simple arithmetic, but

that was never to be.

Then you introduced me to your cousin geometry,

who had all of these issues--always trying to find a new angle,

obsessed with shapes and degrees of separation. We got on ok, but

I refused to let myself get close,

fool me once and all that.

Next trig. Then calculus

I knew that holding back had been apropos.

Words like derivatives, integrals and limits

That I'm pretty sure you made up Math as a last stab at cruelty.

What happened to you?

Only talk to you now during grocery store trips

When we'll run into each other discussing the cost effectiveness

Of a bag of apples versus cookies.

(Cookies always win btw.)

We'll never be the same again.

# Running with Scissors into Paradise

Problems stick to the soles

of worn sneaker tread,

Following behind,

Picking pockets of hope,

Filling them with failed expectations,

Empty bellies.

But doesn't destitution taste

Better on a sunny beach?

Does life have to stand

where you fall?

When did it stop being adventures

And just be running away?

What age is the stop gap limit

For living your dreams?

# Secret Gatekeeper

Weight of secrets kept

Were thick gold bars

Hanging from a noose around the neck.

Swallowing may choke you,

One more bar may break you.

Taking you.

Paralysis.

Suspended state of animation.

Poker face

Never so strong.

Freshly laid cement,

Feet solidified in the center.

Won't repeat.

# Faith Unloaded

Finding daybreak banging on this damn keyboard

lamenting on how this shouldn't be it.

Is this all ya get?

The end-all be-all of existence.

A step up from abject poverty.

Empty rooms.

Endless lost dreams and the losing end of hope.

Who's to blame?

The failing market,

loss of a stable economy,

the rose dysfunction of childhood,

"selfless" acts for others' welfare?

the constant working toward something, anything

but always holding back

because faith ran dry years ago,

like pension checks

And that feeling of life being possible,

Positivity in the fruitlessness of being.

# Snow Falls

Her head filled with nonsense,

candy-coated memories laced with daffodils and frilly things.

She thought he could do no wrong.

She thought he could right her wrongs.

She thought wrong.

The girl turned woman-child dragged her left foot when she walked.

Holdover from the broomstick from that one time...

when the sand still sparkled like diamonds

and the sky was still filled with stars and UFOs.

So much unknown.


Snow blinded her brown-eyed blues,

Wind stole her breath in puffs.

Red pea coat missing three buttons.

She holds the collar up, breathes inside, fails to warm her.

But her thoughts, inflamed her.

Last night he'd ridden her like he was a rock star

and she was his sweetest melody.

And her body sang to his, and his shouted the chorus.

Though he'd whispered his mom's name in her ear.

Those things happened.


Before he was limp, he'd pulled out.

She hadn't quite reached her crescendo,

but she'd milked him for every drop.

Wishing to make this duet last forever.

She'd let his essence dry inside her thighs.

Needing anything of his.


And he'd held her afterwards.

For a minute.

Then he'd rolled over and snored.


He'd forgotten to pick her up today.

Only had three more blocks to go.

Lips cracked and bleeding.

Fingers in the sleeves.


She recalled when his eyes had met her across the bar,

and he'd nodded and winked.

She was over before it began.

He'd told her that she would do for the night.

But she had to be out by dawn.


And she did and she had.

And she did and she had.

She had did it like she was Burger King,

And he'd had everything his way.


Two more blocks.

The Shaping of an "Angry" Black Woman 68

# Part Four

*Caught between an aftermath*
*and an after mint.*

The Shaping of an "Angry" Black Woman 70

# Baby's Daddy Blues

Tell the world that drinks have inspired you to be thorough.

You want to keep it really, really, real though.

You should know this shit has got to go.

You've been living up in my house.

Kissing my son's face,

while your lips have been down in some nasty, triflin' place.


What? What's that?


You ain't got nothin' to say?

Your transgressions got you wishing for

a relationship attorney or a rent-an-alibi lie

Let me put you on Facebook blast

About a past never seems to stop haunting

your sorry ass.


*Public Service Announcement:*

*Bitches do be crazy,*

*and this bitch is crazy*

*if she thinks I'm not going to crack her skull*

*have a talk with her.*

*Hope she enjoyed the food stamps he gave her.*

*The rock she smoked.*

*Obviously she's one of those bitches,*

*giving brain for that ghetto champagne*

*a 40 of Old E and a box of Newports.*

*If the sky was falling,*

*She'd have her glass pipe to the ready.*

*Never see her raggedy ass run so fast*

*til the Man drives pass.*

*Giving up pussy for money, or gas*

*Sad.*


My patience is dry,

Like your Mama's meatloaf.

Yeah, she can get some too.

She never did accept

That I was your boo

Maybe she knew more than I do.


What can't look me in the eye?


It's good she knows her son so well.

Then she knows her home is about to go to Hell.

But mine will be ruled with peace and silence.

No more violence, headaches or drugs.

Take that bag, be gone,

Don't worry, he'll forget you before long.

## Love Song

*When I was a child,*

I took to your affections,

soaking up every drop of

your words. The ground, me,

you, the rain, filling my

every reservoir. Growing me.

Nurturing.


*I spake as a child,*

I hear these words--I love you,

As they tremble from your tongue,

Sliding over my body

Leaving only a residue in their wake.

It's all too easy for you.


*I understood as child*

You love? You. Love. Me?

You can't possibly love me and

sleep with her or him or them.

You can't love me.

While being dishonest, disrespectful,

and leaving me disheartened,

Disillusioned.


*I thought as a child, but when I became a woman*

Love to you is little more than a word, beginning a phrase to tickle your fancy.

So you can get those panties to drop.

Get your tip wet, and break her off a little somethin' somethin.'

Nine months later, you're just a face in the rearview mirror,

Dodging custody hearings and putting on some Lil Wayne

Getting ready for the club.


*I put away childish things.*

You disregard protection like prophylactics were invented

just to make sex feel bad.

This is not the 70s, your excuses, though varied, are invalid.

The love you don't feel is inherent in those sweet words

you whisper to me, she, they, See above.

I'll miss you, when you're gone,

But I dismiss you.

*Inspired by Corinthians I Verse 2 Chapter 1*

# The Greatest Show on Earth

Step right up, ladies and gents, and feast your eyes.

The greatest caretaker ever known.

At your service.

If there's a problem, a situation, some malady in your fallacy,

She will deal you into her world and sit out this hand.

Because you need attention,

And she can wait.

She'll be here all day.

She feeds off you to nourish her broken center.


But enough about her.


You, there in the front.

You look entirely damaged, filled with mommy issues.

Don't you want to date her,

counseling or any type of therapy?

No. Of course. Why make an effort to receive help,

when you're so obviously unhinged?

What was I thinking?

No worries or judgment here.

Come closer you beautifully broken toys.

She'll glue you together piece by piece.

She can rebuild you.

She can make you stronger.

Her? Who is she? Let's talk about you.

Yes, by all means, she lives for commitment-phobes,

the semi-straight—*you know, only straight if enough liquor hasn't been poured yet,*

sexual issues (don't like too much, like too much, only wanna bang you in the butt),

drinkards, druggies

worldwide social misfits.

You sir, do you often suffer from whiskey dick?

Then come on down!

Hey you over there,

do you have problems functioning in given social situations

unless on a drug prescribed by Louie down the street?


Have a seat, she'll be with you shortly.



Have you ever had sex with a woman

then afterward told her that you liked her like a sister?

...a sister for crying out loud, then give her a call.

step right up, take a bow.

Your mental issue, she needs it right now.

# Written Revenge

When the boy hurts the girl,

Her world's revolutions stop.

She can't see beyond,

Caught between afterthought and after mint.

No trade backs.


Mouth tightens, bold.

Her fingers predatory,

flying across the keys.

Raging against the machine.

The mechanism that held her back,

No trade backs.


Angry word here.

Terse word there.

Tear in the eye.

A tear on the heart

dangling from her sleeve.

His protests are ignored.

She's unstoppable.

Filled with self-righteous anger

and self-hating bullshit.

Hiding behind veneer of honesty and truth.

Each word sharpened to precision.

Needing to take her pound of flesh.

No trade backs.


She's never been one for half-measures.

Half-true.

All self-righteous anger

Self-hating bullshit.

And she can't say what made it go wrong.

She wants.

She needs.

She feels.

She can't see beyond

her scrapes and bruises.

Just as selfish as she

accused him to be.


He made her feel loved

and invisible.

Dichotomy breaking down ego

and self-confidence.

Her emotions too bruised


for exposure.

Until that night,

when she felt less than zero.

She broke the seal.

And she let the words fly.

No trade backs.


Just because,

Just because.

In her mirror universe,

he wants her to cease to exist.

He'll erase her from his cell,

deleted from Facespaces

No trade backs.

She can't chip his stone wall of silence.

It tightens in her throat.

Too loud to be told.

She wanted to be everything to everyone.

She wanted to be his everything.

His someone.


She's waiting for him.

She self-mutilates internally.

And she wants to be his eternally.

# The Stranger

You looked down into that glass of scotch

Like you were decoding ancient hieroglyphics

and the answers were burned under clinking ice.

Tangible waves and I wanted to share the burden with you.


To press your furrowed brow against my chest,

To be the balm against the stinging blow you'd been dealt.

I didn't know your name,

Yet.


But I knew she'd hurt you.

I hadn't heard the timbre of your voice,

but I know the pitch of your despair,

wanted to add my melodies to your sad song,

taking the blues into a glorious chorus of joy.


We hadn't touched,

but when we do the seas will part,

tsunamis will cease,

my brown eyes will turn blue.

The world forever changed.

I don't know you,

but I do know that the world only

gives you so many options

and my only choice is you.

And then our eyes meet.

# Playing Nice

He--Infatuated with my poetry.

My words.

Can I be so bold as to say,

he will gravitate to less intelligence,

less spark,

just less,

because her smaller waist,

smaller expectations,

just small.

"What do you think?" he kept asking me.

What do I think?

What do you want to know?

What do you want me to say?

Tell me now.

Unable to speak in safe platitudes,

I keep silent.

He thinks me timid.

No, never that.

Just wary, achingly wary.

As with all things

that sound too good.

I'm pretty sure he'd be bad for me.

And he walked home with a copy of my poetry.

# Intrigue

How does he look

Laid out on garden fresh roses

Covered in our sweat?

He's playing me,

I'm a pawn on his arm,

And he's the chess master.

His talent's immense,

He could take me in three moves

And I'd gladly let him castle my queen.

It's been over a week.

An obsession.

Thinking of him 24/7.

He wants to break me.

The idea is sweet

with surprise underneath.

Commanding, domineering,

submitting.

The Shaping of an "Angry" Black Woman 92

# The Birth of Soul

I want to expel your wisdom from my insides,

let my abdomen expand to the fullness of your politics.

My dormant maternal instincts gears to life with a suddenness,

presses the air from my lungs,

my inner thighs quiver in anticipation.

Mind whispers to use caution,

protect myself,

but my womb contracts as your voice,

whiskey soaked and $3 packs of cheap cigarettes roughened,

penetrates my every orifice,

bridging this gap between my stark lifeless reality.

Pressing deep with words of alternative universes,

elevated consciousness dipped and tinged with crude levity
and a frank disregard

for my need to keep my senses.

As the angels and demons, who dance in your head

slip from your tongue,

into my bloodstream,

intoxicating me, and my heart races.


Infusing me with their lusty visions of nirvana,

And my mortal soul weeps.

My breasts grow heavy and warm

With your stylized world.

Tapping into my ovaries.

Your rich timbers triggering my eggs,

Traveling down my fallopian tubes,

matriculating as your words

move like light beams

wiggling infusing my womb

With you.


I feel the spark, as your ideas take root deep inside of me,

growing, stretching, reaching,

taking me to the pinnacle and beyond.

Beyond where sanity lives,

and I grow full with opinions,

your fiery rants, skewed view,

and I have to expel them,

I grab a pen,

Clench my teeth, bearing down,

pushing beyond my limits,

self-imposed boundaries,

And I scrawl, grunting,

sweating in

this damn heat,

Until I birth these words.

The Shaping of an "Angry" Black Woman 96

# Part Five

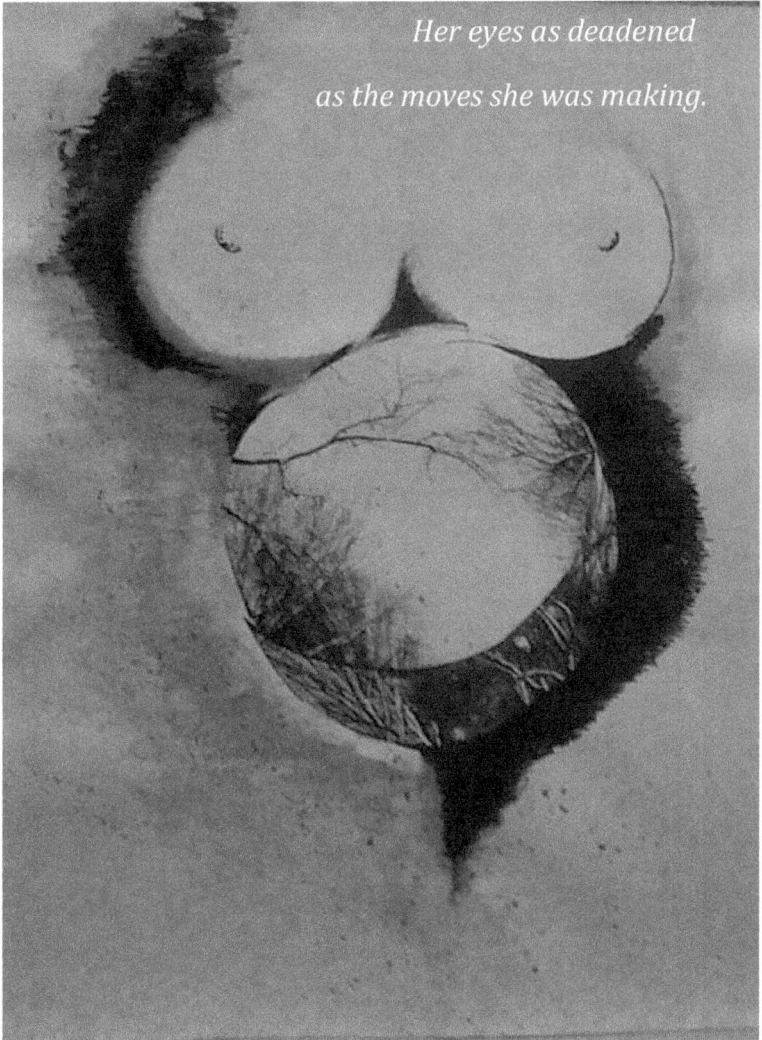

*Her eyes as deadened as the moves she was making.*

The Shaping of an "Angry" Black Woman 98

# The Child Who Never Was

I didn't know I wanted you until I wasn't sure if I could have you.

I see your face in every light-skinned big-eyed little mini-man on The Bus.

I hear your giggle—well his giggle, but it's your giggle,

and I wanna know the secret behind them.


I'm a Facebook stalker,

envious of friends' widening waistbands,

their steady diet of complaints:

too many doctor's visits, bathroom visits, in-law visits, but not enough friend visits.

I scoff at them, smirking on my throne of freedom,

Which I fear may be a misnomer.


If freedom is having the ability to choose,

the flexibility of options, weighting pros and cons

willfully deciding to exercise your free will,

What if your body chooses con

And doesn't bother to consult you?

Your temple has betrayed you in such a fundamental way,

that even though blood flows monthly,

No seeds can be planted here.

Are you truly free?


I didn't know I wanted you until I wasn't sure if I could have
you.

And now I torture myself with the talk with my Man

Who definitely doesn't want you,

I flip through my Rolodex of "what-ifs" because my mind can't
stop thinking.


If my land lay barren, a mockery of femininity,

where once something could have lived,

may have lived, but time marches on, and life happens.

And so nothing will happen here.

Wasn't the purpose to breed, be fruitful and multiply?

If I can't, is my body a testament against God?

"I have good news! My daughter is pregnant!"

says the lady sitting across from me on The Bus,

even as I pen these words.

And the little boy in his suspenders and gap-toothed grin,

I can see your face in his.

I didn't know I wanted you until I wasn't sure I could have you,

but the thought of you makes me heavy with possibilities that may never be.

# Post-Op

Weak. Exhausted.

As yet unfamiliar with this body.

Gentle turn of stomach,

soft nooks and sumptuous valleys

inexplicable hardness now.

Marred with a misshapen, angry line drawn

divots, oozing nooks

Render me lonely,

touch-free zone.

Phantom razor claws hook

my thighs during the five hour tour of my insides.

They scrape against

nerve endings, possibly

grinding lit charcoal in when I'm not looking.

That could be the source of the burning sulfur

as opposed to an over-active imagination.

But why then are the spots where my thighs meet

so cold, it's like they're foreign entities

rumbling against each other?

Sitting up pushes out rivulets of molten magma,

pooling in the recesses of my stomach.

When did rolling over ever hurt like this?

# Doctor's Sensitivity

Touch my pregnant tumor belly,

I demanded rubbing stomach against

his shoulder.


I'm fat already,

When I lean back a little

And pay my tummy lovingly,

I receive those awkward, "When are you due?" questions.

Already.


I'm due for a beer at Noon-thirty.

Is that what you mean?

I'm due for another degree in about two years if my poor health

And self-sabotaging tendencies can be reined in.

I'm due to have these seething vestiges removed from my uterus

Five weeks from now,

Fifteen days from now,

Five days from now.

Now.


"Did you know you can bleed to death from these?"

Another awkward, yet more accurate question.

She gave the asking the same consideration

that one would give the weather or finding a sock's mate.

Dead. Bleeding.

Idly thought

"Oh you want to *keep* your uterus? Well you better start having kids today!"

"Did you know that at 33 you're less likely to be able to get pregnant?

At 35 it drops more

And 40 it drops even further."


Actually, I did know that.

I also know that at 20, I was too busy being a college kid to raise one.

At 25, I was too busy denying love to make one.

At 30, I was just regarding my nether regions as more than a pleasure palace.

"Did you know your uterus is the size of someone 5 months pregnant?

Did you know, you should get it all taken out, because you're not using it anyway?"


Hey Doctor Sensitivity,

Did you know laying laid back,

Legs spread,

Feet in stirrups

(Open a little wider please.)

Makes you feel absolutely powerless?

Did you know that shoving those cold paddles inside of me hurts?

Did you know that fertility is a subject to be handled as gently

As the newborn that I may or may not be able to have?


Hey Doctor Sensitivity,

Have you ever felt your ovary on the outside of your body?

Because you're not supposed to.

It should be like a liver or a kidney, you know it's there intuitively,

But otherwise it does its job in silence.

Do you know what's like to have the daily wakeup call of aches and pains,

Where insides feel shredded and battered,

The pain leveling the back, down into the thighs through the knees,

if you twist wrong,

Move too fast,

Stretch too much,

Your body snaps you back to reality,

And you try to disguise the whimper as a cough?


Do you know what it feels like to know your body has tricked itself

Believing a source of malignant cells a source of life.

But the only thing you're carrying is your body's latest trial,

Worse than getting fat or when you stopped growing tall.

Did you know that fear tastes like pennies,

which taste like blood,

so you may be divesting yourself of years of stored fear,

if life were a poem and almost bleeding out a metaphor for living.

The Shaping of an "Angry" Black Woman 110

# WoW Widow

I can't compete with epic weaponry,

You and your friends going on raids,

robbing awesome bases.

Exploring a world filled with orcs that evening endorses.

Maybe if I had the body of a Blood Elf...


If only I could raise your health level,

it wouldn't be just me and your cat,

streaming YouTube videos,

while your guild has LAN parties and

your boys makes sure to have a priest to revive you,

so you can kill The Boss.


I'm just a n00b.

A lonely n00b.

IRL.

I'm not nerdy enough.

I prefer industrial to Math Rock,

and Jay-Z to nerdcore.

I don't understand astrophysics

and I prefer to meet people in

person than via the internet.


My mind works in a purely illogical manner.

Numbers shift in and out of focus.

But I can tell you when there's a rainbow somewhere

because that sky has the golden cast,

And the air weighs sweetly on your glasses.

And I hate to say it but--

<<*I like Star Trek better than Star Wars*>>

There, I said it.

I found it sophomoric,

Even before Lucas came back and

ruined the franchise

and sold his soul for Jar Jar Binks.

Can't wait for the Disney made action figures.

But the worse part of all--

I moved out last week,

And you didn't notice.

# Ink's Pain

Ink stains my hand's side,

A roadmap to the evolution of my Truth.

Plotting the course when my body chose

between tomorrow and only yesterday

when blood clots ran due north

to hapless lungs.

I never knew what dying felt like,

unless oxygen was crowded from

those empty sacs,

And reality narrowed to my fingertips

gripping your arm.

Reminding me that my Truth

had led me to you.

# Ace Boon Coon

She cupped that turkey death.

Ice clinking against the glass,

"They can't give anymore.

It's got to stop someday. "

I nodded.


We are partners.

Though snow driven angels must have kept us around for my birthday.

Or all them white girls hanging around for hers.

Remember playing gas games?

I got four dollars, almost half of a fourth of a tank.


*I need to drive to work.*

*60 minutes roundtrip;*

*I might make it.*

*Wish me luck.*

It's hard to let it go.


A stripper was on the pole beside of us,

Her eyes as deadened as the moves she was making,

I could play her ribs like a harpsichord.

Some of the notes would be flat.

She took a last drink and then reared back

Four shelves,

Crash boom-oh shit-dash.


It seemed so less when it starts,

The self-destruction

Sinks in and

So cloudy followed by the remorseful couch

Junkie Sundays.

We've done wrong.

We must lay on this couch and feel terrible,

and say well at least we didn't try to sell nobody's kids for crack.

Damn.

Thank you Intervention for normalizing our dysfunction.


A Man big like Negro Mountain

Bald head should be leading

Him to a sandwich,

Descending, unlike the foot

Rising to connect to her ass.

DJ Stripper's jaw dropped but scrambling toward Exit sign like nirvana.

We were so thirsty.


And the connection

Grew to an unreal proportion.

Travel only seems to push that envelope.

Now, I have to give birth to a turkey-sized tumor.

My uterus has misshapen itself to all proportions.

Through rotting teeth

Childhood baggage

And children acting out of pocket in the hood.

United by misery and love.


How does this doorknob work again?

And with a nudge and shove,

We escape into the rain.

Into the wilderness.

Laughing that we'd made it to the other side.

# Part Six

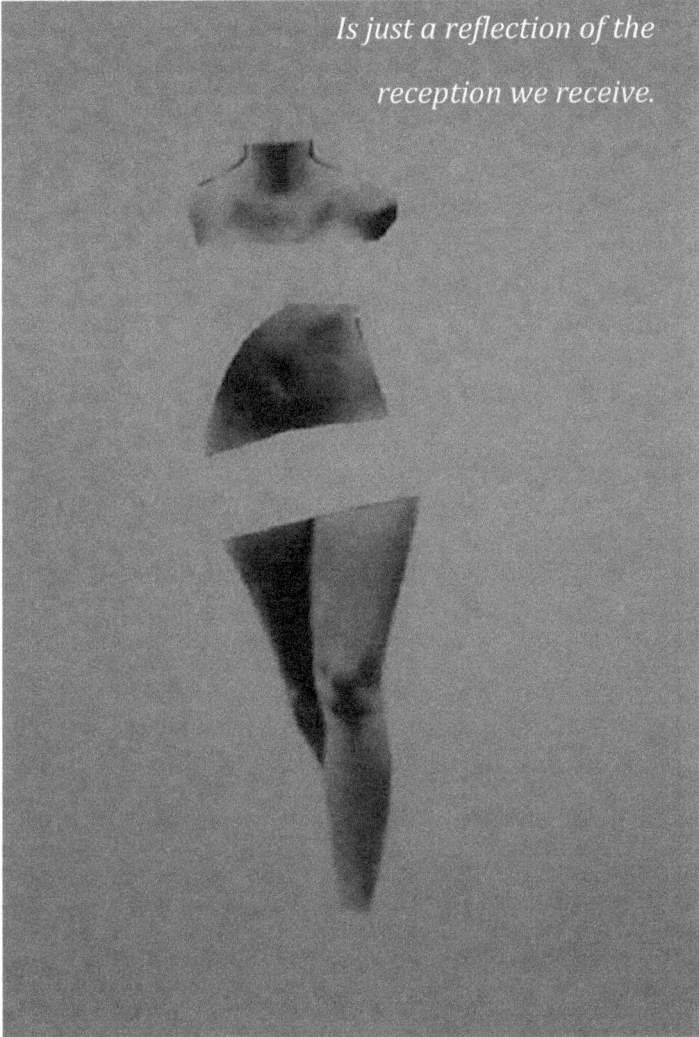

*Is just a reflection of the reception we receive.*

The Shaping of an "Angry" Black Woman 122

# Hot Comb-Self- Deception

Skin tones denotes my worth
Is best expressed by
How straight hair is pressed.
These nappy roots an affront to all the
Tamed-hair women trying to keep it
100 by showing physical expression of oppression, chemical
lies
Destroying ties to the distant past.
"You know girl, you can get your hair done here."
Like these follicles are in some state of suspended animation,
Waiting for the penetration of the no lye lie shattering the
hair's strong curvature,
Lies limp against my face.
Lifeless.

She knows about it.
Gold medals hang from neck,
International super-star, middle podium key.
Sacrificing youth, body, family to live that
American dream of winning at all costs.
Bold hater; old mindset
Won't break the mold.
Say she can't rep right, cuz her hair ain't tight.
You must be beyond all reason,
All seasons revolve around the hair type.
This is question of your racist perception of what your race
should look like,

which is more white?

She's on TV. She tells me
The weather for 20 some years, now trading stories
On the unemployment line.
Her gently curved head, proud, sits on swan-like neck.
Cocoa butter perfection, harkening back to
Nefertiti.
She shears her chemical compost,
Tendrils fall from her now naked crown.
Just as a beautiful. Just as strong.
Just as fired, for doing it wrong they say she is too much man,
Her essence of femininity
Was nestled in those shorn locks of conformity.

My eau de Sundays were Blue Magic and burnt hair.
Front-porch, still my hair fresh pressed, hot comb
Sizzled and popped from the gas stove
Until the heat fired from the hot metal comb.
Like Icarus flying too close to the sun,
But the sun was flying beside me.
Sizzle, burn, got that ear again.
And then it was the chemical, forcing my hair into ways of life
that it knew not.
Take the back of the comb and smooth it,
Smooth it.
Make you into something whiter and brighter.
At least you don't have one of those Shaniqua names.
You can pass on an application.
Oiling, oily, curly, straightening,

The process of hair was a process that I didn't care.
My Barbie ways had passed me.
I was ready for change.
So I stopped.
Stopped curling, pressing, processing,
Stripping it, coaxing it,
Forcing it into an unnatural poker straight state.
Breaking off at the ends in protest.
Now it grows wild and free as the trees.
When I pick it out sometimes I think it may in fact touch the moon.
It's a thing of wonder.
It is me.

# An Ode to Hip Hop

Hip hop occupied the music industry
having people's attention on lockdown.
Black community a state of emergency.
Anthems demands attention; people stand up.
This is my world
and it's ugly
and it's raw.
Know its existence.
Behind the wide-eyed innocence of an electric youth.
Video Killed the Radio Star, but it destroyed the reality years
later.
Not the prompted, digitally enhanced Jersey Housewives
hoarding teen pregnancies for an intervention.
No, the reality of strong syncopated beats
where words are like life gnashing against teeth
and the sounds had the pop-pop-pop like guns shooting down
your ignorance.
"Thinking of a master plan,
but ain't nothin' but sweat inside my hand."
Remember that what remains is like the shattered
misinformation
Melly Mel didn't drop The Message
because it had a phat beat for booty shaking.
He didn't tell you he was close to the edge,
because man sitting behind desk wears suit and tie
sign away your life on the dotted line,
you'd be rewarded with all the bitches and hoes you can shake
your dick at,

as long as you perpetuated the myth that every rapper's getting rich or dying trying.

I'm talking to you.

Hip hop, you were the love of my life,

You were the shining nugget of truth in this cloying cacophony of rainbows and butterfly dreams

and kids on the New Wave stream.

You were what a nosey little sister found in her brother's tape deck

--A cassette tape is an item used in ancient times, like the 80s, to record music and for lovelorn deejays to express their amour on a mixed tape.--

It's a perpetual slippery slope, where folks get it twisted, slapping down opponents faster than potential Baby Daddy's on Maury.

I'm sorry, you are the father.
Shhheeeeit.
I told you Jaquandre looked just like you!

You've persistently stroked yourself into delusions of grandeur and glory.

You're having a bukkake play date with every daughter and mother in America.

And they smile as you call them bitches and hoes.

And they dance their hardest when you go the farthest teaching them how to drop it like it's hot

Your misogyny dripping from their chins. Shiny on their grins.

When once a Queen asked you,

"Who you calling a bitch?"

I hope this ain't where the story ends.

Maybe hip hop is now like fashion,
This style too will die
And then people will be forced to remember.

# A Step Outside Your Box

You're a very civic-minded citizen, Mr. America.
You pay your taxes on time.
Believe in separation of church and state.
I can see the flag waving in the reflection of your Rolex.
You even have a friend who is Black.
And you can't help but ask me.
What's it like to fuck a Black woman?
Don't be offended, you say, licking your lips.
Like being with an alien with better hair, I say.
Like every fantasy you've ever had, but darker, I say.
Why are you so angry, Black woman?

You're very active in your community, Mrs. America.
You're on the PTA.
You volunteer at the Soup kitchen.
You support your husband every week.
You're nails are done by the Asian girls gleaming in the light.
We have a Black president now.
Racism is over.
You don't deserve reparations.
Blacks are too lazy as it is.
You were probably sold by your tribe to get here.
Tribal feuds or whatever.
Why are you so angry Black woman?

There you are, Little America.
You 're in the little league.
A boy scout to boot.

Blonde hair gleams like a halo
When light shines on you,
As your tiny fingers to those pictures,
Unerring in its aim.
Five figures--lightest to darkest,
On the page.
He's bad, because he's darker.
He's stupid because he's darker.
He's nicer, because he's lighter.
Why are you so angry, Black Woman?

Why does my fist ball in impotent rage?
Why do you feel that an elected official of a certain hue negates
my experience, Mrs. America?
Why are you afraid when you look at me, Little America?
I indulge in fantasies of what life would be, if you were me.
If you listened instead of judged.
Heard my truth.
Walked in these Chucks.
Saw me more than an amusement or a fuck.

## Blind Eye

Expansion constricted,
Ankle shackles clank when I'm shufflin'.
Every day struggling.
How can you worry about first-world problems,
Like not getting in line for the new Apple drop,
When hunger has your stomach grinding,
Sour saliva coats your mouth,
You feel so weak.
Choosing between utilities and meds,
Turn the gas off for the summer,
Then I'll get a few churches to pay in the fall,
Have it back on before snow flies.
Step one in living this life.
Going to ER for this hacking in my chest,
Lingers on for months,

Cain't get no rest.
Got two jobs,
Minimum wages,
Maximum labor.
Still picking up canned goods at food banks
To fill these cupboards.
I make too much for food stamps.
99 percent? Who's got time for math?
This is the forgotten percent.
The poor working class.
Sciatic nerve is acting up.
Feels like fire running down my back.
Burning through my resolve to just keep on.
Keeping on.
Still wishing my baby's daddy
Would come through with some diapers.

Or babysitting.
At least a birthday call to one of your kids.
Guess it's hard to keep track of all of them.
Be merry.
Kids love ya.
You're like Santa Claus,
Fiction that I made up so they think
someone other than me cares.
System loves ya.
Still waiting for that child support to kick in.
Five years later.
I'm still cleaning up after ya.
Gotta bust out these dishes real quick,
Kiss mom so I can go.
Time is another luxury I don't have.

# Pudding Pop Revolution

They liked him better when he was selling pudding pops.
Wearing his motley colored sweaters
Sitting by his TV daughter's bedside
making airplane engine sounds to get her to
take her medicine.
Lip-synching to "Night and Day."
Contorting his face into a loveable ugly mask.

When he laid down his wrath,
Grandfather fed up, disgusted,
disapproval over his grandchildren's follies.
Watching them become a parody of themselves,
and living the dream record companies were selling to them.

Now a pariah to these younger generations,
Selling out his Black brethren.
You wanted a pat on the head.
Acknowledgment that everything moving right along
to the masses keep these failures a secret
Don't give racists anchors to latch.

Life does not come with a laugh track.
This man is not your father,
more of your scolding uncle three sides removed,
Treat him with respect.
He only says it because he loves you.
It hurts him to see what you've become.
He wants you to soar, exploring the dark in your life unfiltered
Pushing beyond the limitations society has placed upon you
Discovering the you that you didn't know existed.

Outside cold, steel bars,
In the arms of the woman you got pregnant
Teaching your daughter that beauty is deep
but education is the way to leave here.
And we'll find the way.
Any means necessary to get you to a next level that I can't be at.
Ever vigilant of your messages verbalized
Your hard-won freedoms.
Never forgetting your history
And knowing the elders are always watching.

# The Shaping of an Angry Black Woman

Tired of the accusations,
Slant-eyed gaze as I walk through your stores,
Hearing the lock click on your car door,
You mean to tell you couldn't lock your door before I got here?
You saw me coming.
You wanted to make sure I know that you're prepared for my
nefarious scheme to
Perform a smash and grab in your two-toned Cutlass Supreme.
You want me to feel those tumblers shifting and sliding,
So I can't take these groceries filling my hands and do what,
exactly?
Bash you with this deadly lettuce?
Black people will steal anything you know.

Enough of your predetermined notions of my presumed
intelligence
Based on solely on the percentage of melatonin in my
complexion.
I'm not an inner-city dropout with a glass pipe with one hand, a
baby diaper in the other,
Name filled with awkwardly placed Qs and apostrophes.
Unless my crackhead tendencies are getting in the way of
yours, it's none of your concern.
Mind your own.
I'm also not some basketball wife who has more money and
time to burn than sense.

Enough blaming me for what you think Obama

Should or shouldn't have done.
I haven't shaken an angry finger at you for every other
president's foibles and fuck-ups
because you share the same pasty skin tone.
Your assumption that I voted him into office based primarily
on his skin color and my need for welfare is asinine.
Who did I vote for? you ask.
Mind your own.
My ballot is not for your public consumption.
That's why we vote behind a booth
And not in the middle of market square with a show of hands.

Oh, and guess what? I do tip.
But my tips are based solely upon how pleasant, prompt and
efficient your service is.
If I only leave you a dollar, it's not because
Black people don't know how to tip.
You looked at me, decided my black hands would not show my
appreciation of your service,
And your performance reflected that.
Your rude, short and generally unpleasant behavior was
reflected with the unhappy emoticon I drew on the receipt.
You made an off-handed comment about me not skipping out
on the check,
You're lucky all I did was give you a George Washington
instead of a Buster Douglass.
But then I would've shown out publicly
Isn't that what's expected from the angry black woman?
Weaves and fake nails flinging in a clamor of
"oh no you didn'ts."

"Why do Black people get to use the n-word and I can't?"
I'd like to postulate a different question:
Why do you presume that all black people use the "n" word?
My life is not represented by rap videos.
I do not want to "reclaim" a word that was never mine from get.
Labels someone else slapped on me and I'm supposed to use it
The difference between the "er" and the "a" standing between a
Fist bump and a fist bumping your face.

"Why am I so touchy?"
I'm just tired.
Bone-deep weary of playing this game,
Where everyone blames everyone else for their problems.
Somehow I stole your jobs,
But I'm too lazy to work,
So I'm taking all the welfare,
All the food stamps,
Though you get the most.

Maybe the angry Black woman
Is just a reflection of the
reception we receive.
Your need to have a villain in your life.
In the cowboy flicks, he wore the black hat.
Here, we just wear Black skin.

# ABOUT THE AUTHOR

Tamara is a soulful poet, blogger, and social networker. She has been surviving life since the late 70s and started writing poetry in the 90s to get her through the 2000s. Fortunately, that still seems to be working. She runs her web site PenPaperPad where she discusses all things writing. She was published in Empirical Magazine's first poetry book, "Latitude on 2nd," and received Honorable Mention: WV Writer's Conference Poetry Division. She also been a featured poet for several events including African American Arts and Heritage Academy, a FEM fundraiser and Take Back the Night-domestic violence awareness event. She was the co-organizer of Morgantown Poets and the creator of Tha.Speakeasy, a monthly spoken word event in Morgantown, WV among others. Her career has also had a special focus and attention to the social struggles of people with disabilities and the homeless. She dedicated two years to being an

AmeriCorps and a VISTA volunteer. She also has experience as a newspaper journalist and an event organizer. She has recently traded the Appalachian Mountains for the sandy beaches of Hawai'i to explore the dynamics of a different region and expand her literary horizons.

She can be reached at: Twitter: @penpaperpad, Facebook: http://facebook.com/TamaraWoodstheWriter and Google+:https://plus.google.com/+TamaraWoods